# POP STARS

## How to Have a Number 1 Single

**Stan Cullimore**

## Contents

illustrated by Tony Forbes

# Getting to Number 1

This is our Number 1 single.

Everyone knows that a Number 1 single is one that goes to Number 1 in the charts.

2

But how does it get there?

We'll tell you!

**FACT**

The charts are changed every week. The people who make up the charts have to find out two things:

1 They have to find out how many copies each CD single has sold in the week.

2 They have to find out how many times the CD single has been played on the radio in the week.

# Get into a band

# Find a song

# Find a manager

Now that you have found the song and the band it is time to find a 'manager'.

Most pop bands have a special person who sorts things out for them. This person is called a manager. It is a very important job

The manager goes to meet people from record companies.

He will tell them that the pop band is going to sell a lot of CDs. If the record company agrees with him, it will offer the pop band a record contract.

12

# Record the song

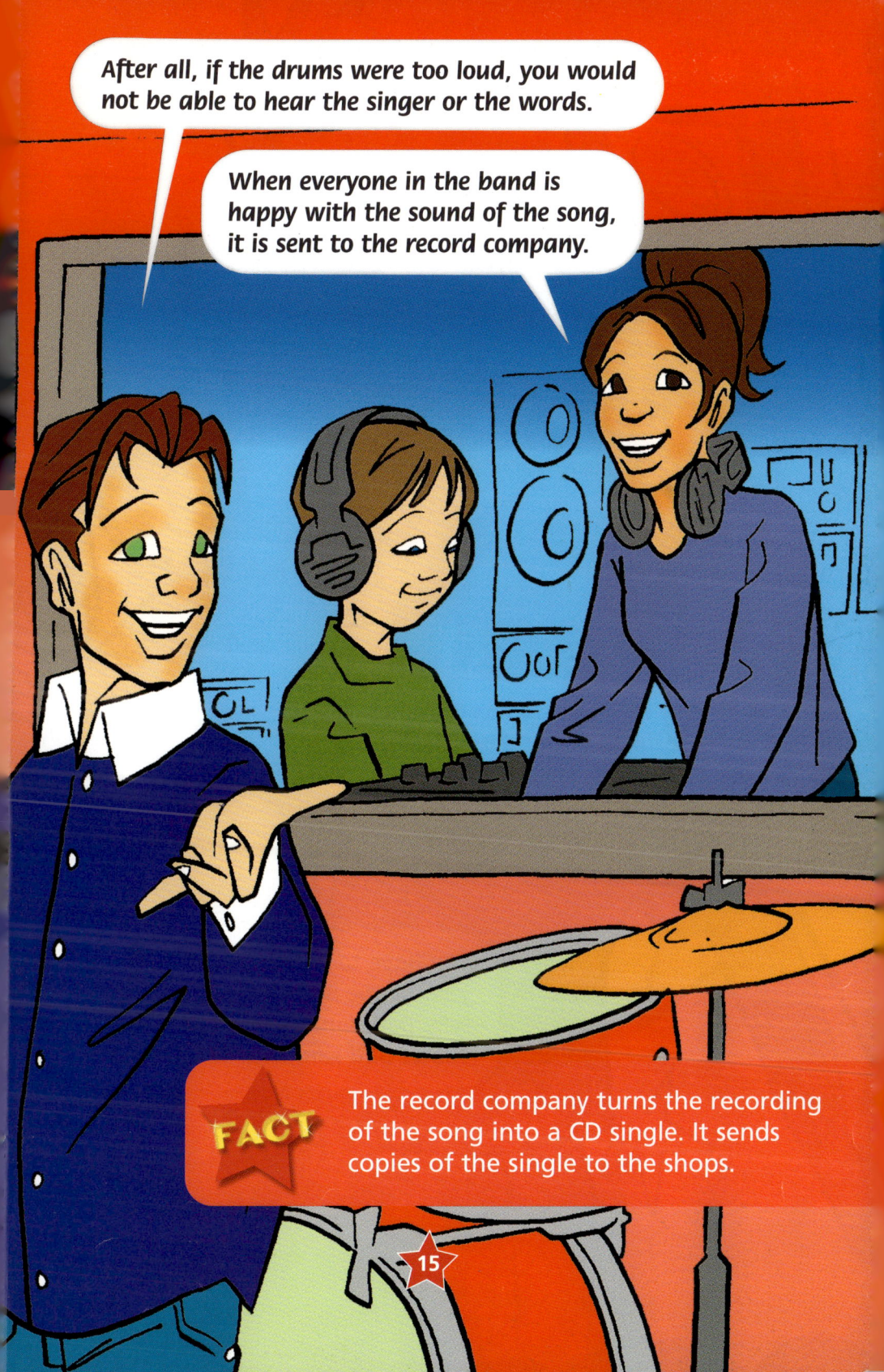

It is all very well having lots of copies of your CD single in the shops, but if no one buys them, then your song will not even get into the charts, let alone get to Number 1!

You have to let people know that your single is in the shops. This is why pop bands go on television shows and sing their latest single.

# You have a Number 1 single!

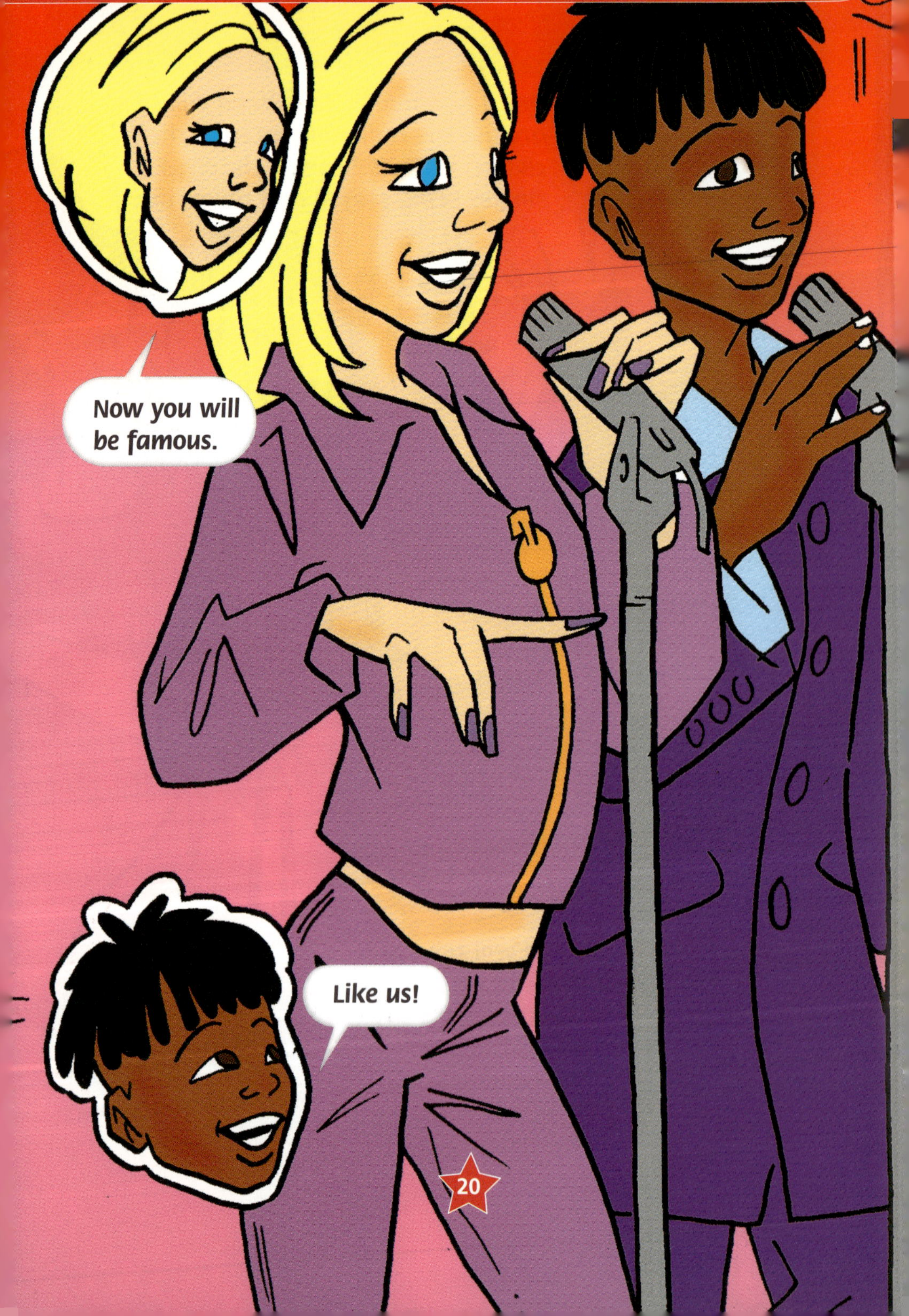

# What next?

I wonder what will happen to us if our next single does not become a Number 1 single?

Will people still shout out our names?

Will they still want to be our fans?

Will they still want us to sign autographs?

I don't know.